MAY 2017

The Crane Loves Grain

Pam Scheunemann

Consulting Editor, Diane Craig, M.A./Reading Specialist

Publishing Company

Published by ABDO Publishing Company, 4940 Viking Drive, Edina, Minnesota 55435.

Printed in the United States.

Credits
Edited by: Pam Price
Curriculum Coordinator: Nancy Tuminelly
Cover and Interior Design and Production: Mighty Media
Photo and Illustration Credits: BananaStock Ltd., Brand X Pictures, Corbis Images, Corel, Eyewire Images, Hemera, Image 100, Tracy Kompelien, PhotoDisc, Stockbyte

Library of Congress Cataloging-in-Publication Data

Scheunemann, Pam, 1955-
    The crane loves grain / Pam Scheunemann.
      p. cm. -- (Rhyme time)
    Includes index.
    ISBN 1-59197-781-9
    1. English language--Rhyme--Juvenile literature. I. Title. II. Rhyme time (ABDO Publishing Company)

PE1517.S4 2004
428.1'3--dc22

                                                                          2004049111

SandCastle™ books are created by a professional team of educators, reading specialists, and content developers around five essential components that include phonemic awareness, phonics, vocabulary, text comprehension, and fluency. All books are written, reviewed, and leveled for guided reading, early intervention reading, and Accelerated Reader® programs and designed for use in shared, guided, and independent reading and writing activities to support a balanced approach to literacy instruction.

Let Us Know

After reading the book, SandCastle would like you to tell us your stories about reading. What is your favorite page? Was there something hard that you needed help with? Share the ups and downs of learning to read. We want to hear from you! To get posted on the ABDO Publishing Company Web site, send us e-mail at:

sandcastle@abdopub.com

SandCastle Level: Fluent

Words that rhyme do not have to be spelled the same. These words rhyme with each other:

complain

pain

crane

plain

Dane

reign

grain

stain

Maine

vane

Tracia likes to read.

So when it's time to go to the library, she does not **complain**.

The national bird of Uganda is the African crowned crane.

Cara and Barbra are eating cereal with their parents.

Cereal is made from **grain**.

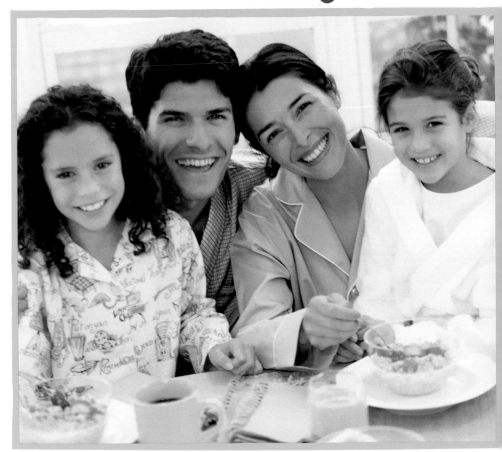

Hamlet is a Great Dane.

Geremy asks his doctor to look at his arm because he is feeling some **pain**.

The Portland Head Light is a lighthouse on the coast of **Maine**.

Doto, Mosi, and their friends live on a **plain** in Tanzania.

The duration of a king's rule is called his **reign**.

Dusty got dirty playing soccer.
He hopes his uniform won't
always have a **stain**.

There is a weather **vane** on top of the barn.

The Crane Loves Grain

Blaine was
a big crane
who lived
way up in Maine.

At a farm
on Penny Lane,
Blaine sat on top
of a weather vane.

15

He thought really hard with his brain,
"How can I obtain
some of my favorite grain?"

Just then Blaine
was joined by his friend Jane,
who was a Dane.

As it started to rain,
Blaine began to explain
to Jane about the grain.

Jane said,
"I know a place
that does contain
some of the
very finest grain!"

Together they flew over the river next to the plain.

The flight was a bit of a strain.

But when they tasted the grain, they knew it was worth the pain.

Blaine said, "Why, this is the best grain!
I sure can't complain!"

Rhyming Riddle

What do you call a long-legged bird that doesn't like to dress up?

Plain crane

Glossary

crane. a tall wading bird with a long neck and bill

Dane. a resident of Denmark or someone with Danish heritage

Great Dane. a breed of very tall dogs with short, smooth coats

plain. a large, flat area of treeless land

strain. extreme or difficult effort, exertion, or work

Tanzania. a country in east Africa

Uganda. a country in east Africa

weather vane. a free-moving device that turns to show the direction of the wind

About SandCastle™

A professional team of educators, reading specialists, and content developers created the SandCastle™ series to support young readers as they develop reading skills and strategies and increase their general knowledge. The SandCastle™ series has four levels that correspond to early literacy development in young children. The levels are provided to help teachers and parents select the appropriate books for young readers.

Emerging Readers
(no flags)

Beginning Readers
(1 flag)

Transitional Readers
(2 flags)

Fluent Readers
(3 flags)

These levels are meant only as a guide. All levels are subject to change.

Publishing Company

To see a complete list of SandCastle™ books and other nonfiction titles from ABDO Publishing Company, visit **www.abdopub.com** or contact us at:
4940 Viking Drive, Edina, Minnesota 55435 • 1-800-800-1312 • fax: 1-952-831-1632